BASEBALL RECORDS THAT WILL BE TOUGH TO BEAT

Cynthia Kennedy Henzel

Mitchell Lane
PUBLISHERS

Mitchell Lane
PUBLISHERS

mitchelllanepub.com

2001 SW 31st Avenue
Hallandale, FL 33009

First Edition, 2026.
Author: Cynthia Kennedy Henzel
Designer: Ed Morgan
Editor: Tammy Gagne

Series: Unbreakable Sports Records?
Title: Baseball Records That Will Be Tough to Beat

Library bound ISBN: 979-8-89260-722-3
eBook ISBN: 979-8-89260-733-9

Photo credits: cover, p. 7, 18, 41, 43, 46, 57 Alamy; p. 4–5 freepik.com; p. 9, 45, 51, 53 Shutterstock; p. 13, 15, 17, 23, 25, 27, 31, 33, 35, 36, 51 wikimedia

CONTENTS

INTRODUCTION

Swinging for HISTORY

It was August 1, 1978. Pete Rose of the Cincinnati Reds was on a 43-game hitting streak, which started on June 14. Fans began paying attention when he got a hit in ten **consecutive** games. They wondered if he might beat the record for the most consecutive games with a hit. At game 29, the current record holder, Joe DiMaggio, predicted, "Someday, someone will break it, and if that's the case, I hope it's Pete Rose."

Rose kept going. Soon he reached 30 games. Then 40. At Fulton County Stadium, fireworks boomed, and 45,000 fans cheered as Rose tied Willie Keeler's 44 consecutive games, which the Baltimore Orioles player reached in 1896. The only record to break now was DiMaggio's 56, set in 1941.

The Reds' next game was in Atlanta, Georgia, against the Braves. In the second inning, Rose hit a hard drive. In a miracle catch, the pitcher managed to snag the ball. In the seventh inning, Rose drove another hard ball. The third baseman caught it.

Now, it was the ninth inning. The Reds had two outs. Rose fouled off two pitches. With a count of 2–2, he got ready for a fastball. But pitcher Gene Garber threw a **changeup**. Rose swung—and missed. The game was over, and so was Rose's chance to break one of the most unbreakable records in baseball.

Pete Rose came close to breaking Joe DiMaggio's record for the most consecutive games.

Baseball Records

Baseball records go back to the early 1800s. However, the official records of Major League Baseball (MLB) go back to 1903 for the National League, and 1905 for the American League. Early records are taken from hand-written game sheets, newspaper accounts, and several books about baseball. But researchers often find errors or new evidence, requiring a change in the records.

Records are also affected by changes to rules or equipment over time. For example, MLB went from playing 154 games per season to 162 games in the early 1960s. This gave players more games to set career records. Despite these extra games, some baseball records have stood for many decades.

SWINGING FOR HISTORY

Major League Baseball has more than a hundred years of official records.

CHAPTER ONE

Cy Young's 511 CAREER WINS

Denton True Young was born in 1867 in Gilmore, Ohio. He grew up on a farm before working as a blacksmith, a job that requires great strength. In 1890, he attended a tryout for a minor league baseball team. Craig Muder writes for the National Baseball Hall of Fame. He quoted Young on the organization's website. "I thought I had to show all my stuff. I threw the ball so hard [I] tore a couple of boards off the grandstand." The grandstand looked like a cyclone had hit it. From then on, he was known as Cy, short for cyclone.

Six months later, the 6-foot, 2-inch (1.88-m) pitcher moved up to MLB with the Cleveland Spiders. In 1901, he moved again to play for the Boston Red Sox. On May 5, 1904, Young made history on the pitching mound for the first time in a game against the Philadelphia Athletics. None of that team's players reached first base. It was the first perfect game in modern baseball.

On July 19, 1910, Young walked onto the mound to pitch the second game of a double-header against the Washington Senators. During the ninth inning, he walked the first Washington hitter. A single to the next hitter sent the first runner across home plate. The score was tied. Young walked the next hitter on purpose, and then took out the next two. This tied the game, sending it into extra innings. It took eleven innings, but Young pitched his 500th winning game. He went on to win 11 more games before he retired in 1911. His total remains a record in the sport.

Cy Young became a legendary MLB pitcher.

During his twenty-two-year career, Young also played for the Cleveland Indians and the Boston Braves. He set the record for the most complete games played at 749. He also set the record for career innings pitched at 7,356. Bob Diskin quoted Young on ESPN. "I never had a sore arm, and I pitched every third day," Young said. "Once I pitched every other day for eighteen days."

Young was elected to the National Baseball Hall of Fame in 1937. In 1956, he was honored by the Baseball Writers Association by having his name given to an annual award for excellence for pitchers. The 2023 Cy Young Award went to Gerrit Cole of New York in the American League and Blake Snell of San Diego for the National League.

Walter Johnson

Whose Record Did Cy Young Break?

Walter Johnson was known as baseball's Big Train. He received the nickname due to his large size. He stood 6 feet, 1 inch (1.85 m) tall and weighed 200 pounds (91 kg). Over his career, Johnson struck out 3,508 batters, a record that stood for fifty years. He pitched 110 shutouts. His 417 career wins over a twenty-one-year career was broken by Cy Young.

Many baseball experts consider Young's career wins an unbeatable record. Few, if any, players have matched Young's power and **stamina**. Young also had a keen understanding of the game. He mastered various pitches, and his opponents had a hard time guessing his next move.

Today, it is rare for a player to pitch a complete game. And few players spend more than two decades in MLB, as Young did. Ralph Longo writes for the Bleacher Report. He says, "Just to put Cy Young's record in **perspective**, let's imagine that a [talented, young player] came into the league tomorrow. For him to break Cy Young's record, he would have to average 20 wins a season, for a whopping 26 seasons."

One of Young's many baseball cards from his two-decade career

CHAPTER ONE

Tarik Skubal

Chasing Young's Record

Tarik Skubal was drafted by the Detroit Tigers in 2018. In 2024, the left-handed pitcher had 18 wins and a 2.39 earned run average (ERA). This is the number of runs a pitcher allows the opposing team to score in nine innings. The MLB average is between 4.0 and 5.0. He had 228 strikeouts. The Tigers' first baseman Spencer Torkelson spoke about Tarik on ESPN. "He's special and he's only just getting started."

CHAPTER TWO

Joe DiMaggio's 56-Game HITTING STREAK

Joe DiMaggio was born in Martinez, California, in 1914. He joined the San Francisco Seals, a minor league team, when he was seventeen. In 1936, he joined the New York Yankees.

DiMaggio had a batting average of .381 in 1939 and .352 in 1940. His most impressive MLB hitting streak began on May 15, 1941. By June 3, he had a hit in 20 consecutive games. By June 17, the number had climbed to 30. DiMaggio remained focused on his team's success when he talked to the *New York Daily News* about his hitting streak on June 25. "If my streak ends . . . with us winning a ball game. That's all that matters."

On June 28, he got to 40. On July 2, DiMaggio faced Red Sox pitcher Dick Newsome in the 5th inning. He smashed the ball over the fence, beating the previous record of 44 games with consecutive games with hits. Then he continued hitting. On July 16, he hit a home run against the Cleveland Indians, bringing his total to 56.

His record ended when he failed to get a hit against the Indians the next day. During his hitting streak, DiMaggio got 15 home runs. He drove in 55 runs. He only struck out five times. The end of the hitting streak didn't slow him down. The next day, he began a 16-game hitting streak. He ended up with a hit in 72 out of 73 games.

Joe DiMaggio was known for his hitting ability.

DiMaggio was also an excellent center fielder. He sailed around fielding balls, leading fans to nickname him "The Yankee Clipper." This was a reference to a great sailing ship. His teammate Yogi Berra was quoted by the National Baseball Hall of Fame. Speaking about DiMaggio's fielding, Berra said, "He never did anything wrong on the field. I'd never seen him dive for a ball, everything was a chest-high catch." In 1947, DiMaggio tied the American League fielding record with only one error in 141 games.

DiMaggio retired in 1951 as a beloved player and a cultural icon. His pop culture status continued to rise when he married Marilyn Monroe, a famous movie actress, in 1954. DiMaggio appeared in commercials and performed charity work until his death in 1999. Following his passing, according to ESPN, sports writer Ira Berkow had this to say about the baseball legend's appeal: "He remains a living symbol of excellence, elegance, and power and, to be sure, gentleness."

Whose Record Did Joe DiMaggio Beat?

William Henry Keeler was born in 1872 in Brooklyn, New York. He was known as Wee Willie Keeler due to his small size. He was 5 feet, 4.5 inches (1.6 m) tall. The left-handed hitter didn't have a lot of power, but he could place the ball where he wanted when he hit it. Keeler played for three New York teams. He was then traded to the Baltimore Orioles in 1894. The next year, he set the record for 44 games with consecutive hits.

DiMaggio's 56-game record is considered one of the most unbeatable in baseball. One reason is that players today are more valued for home runs rather than singles. Plus, players face more pitchers during a game than they did in the past. In 2024, only two active players had attained even a 30-game winning streak.

Jose Altuve

Chasing DiMaggio's Record

Jose Altuve was born in Maracay, Venezuela, in 1990. The Houston Astros baseball camp in Venezuela allowed local players to work out with the team. Altuve kept returning, hoping to be signed by the team. Finally, the Astros gave him a chance. He entered MLB in 2011 as a second baseman for Houston. Estimates state that Altuve has a 78 percent chance of getting a hit each time he bats. DiMaggio had a 77.8 percent chance. Still, the odds of Altuve breaking DiMaggio's record are slim.

CHAPTER THREE

Rickey Henderson's 1,406 STOLEN BASES

Rickey Henderson was born in 1958 in Chicago, Illinois. The left fielder began playing with the Oakland Athletics in 1979. The next year, he broke Ty Cobb's record of 96 stolen bases in one season, extending the total into triple digits with 100. In 1982, Henderson was back at it again, with 130 stolen bases that season. And in 1983, he added 108 to his career total. He is the only player with 100 or more steals in three different seasons. He stole 1,406 bases during his career, the most of any MLB player.

Henderson, nicknamed the Man of Steal, played for nine teams during his time in professional baseball. He threw left-handed but batted right-handed. Being left-footed gave him extra power when pushing off first base. But base stealers aren't just fast and powerful. "That Henderson was able to steal so many bases is largely a testament to his rare blend of speed and on-base **acumen**," wrote Zachary D. Rymer in the Bleacher Report.

Henderson was a friend of Lou Brock, whose record he broke. Steve Wilstein of the Associated Press reported on a discussion between the friends. Brock explained, "In every motion [of a pitcher] there is a trigger point and you have to determine where it is by studying the anatomy of the pitcher, how he moves his knee or shoulder. Once the pitcher crosses that trigger point, he has to throw home. . . . Knowing that simplifies the heck out of it."

It takes speed and knowledge to steal bases.

Henderson left MLB in 2003. He played for some minor league teams before retiring in 2007. He also went down in history as a capable hitter. George Steinbrenner, former chairman of the New York Yankees, wrote about Henderson for the National Baseball Hall of Fame. "There was only one Rickey Henderson in baseball," Steinbrenner stated. "He was the greatest leadoff hitter of all time."

Henderson's stolen base record may never be broken. During his time in baseball, batters tried to make hits to bring in base runners rather than focusing more on home runs. Now, making home runs is a priority. Plus, pitchers now throw faster. At 100 miles per hour (161 kph), a pitch reaches home base in the time it takes to blink. It only takes two seconds for the catcher to throw to second base. A runner must be extremely fast.

Whose Record Did Rickey Henderson Break?

Lou Brock was born in El Dorado, Arkansas, in 1939. He began playing in MLB for the Chicago Cubs in 1962. He was traded to the St. Louis Cardinals in 1964. The left fielder got at least 50 steals each year from 1965 to 1976. He set a season record in 1974, stealing 118 bases. Brock retired in 1979 with 938 career steals.

In 2023, new rules affected attempts to steal. To speed up the game, the number of times a pitcher can try to **pick off** a base runner changed. After two attempts, the pitcher receives a **balk** if he is unsuccessful in throwing out the runner. In addition, the size of MLB bases increased from 15 inches (38.1 cm) to 18 inches (45.72 cm). MLB hoped the larger bases would improve player safety and encourage more stolen-base attempts.

Henderson takes off to steal second in a 1983 game.

Corbin Carroll

Chasing Henderson's Record

Corbin Carroll was born in Seattle, Washington, in 2000. He began playing in MLB in 2022 with the Arizona Diamondbacks. Although the left-handed outfielder is young, he already has an impressive stolen-base record. He set a rookie record with 50 stolen bases in 2023. His success rate is 91.5 percent, meaning he makes 54 of every 59 steals he attempts. The average major league success rate in 2023 was 80 percent.

CHAPTER FOUR

Barry Bonds's 762 CAREER HOME RUNS

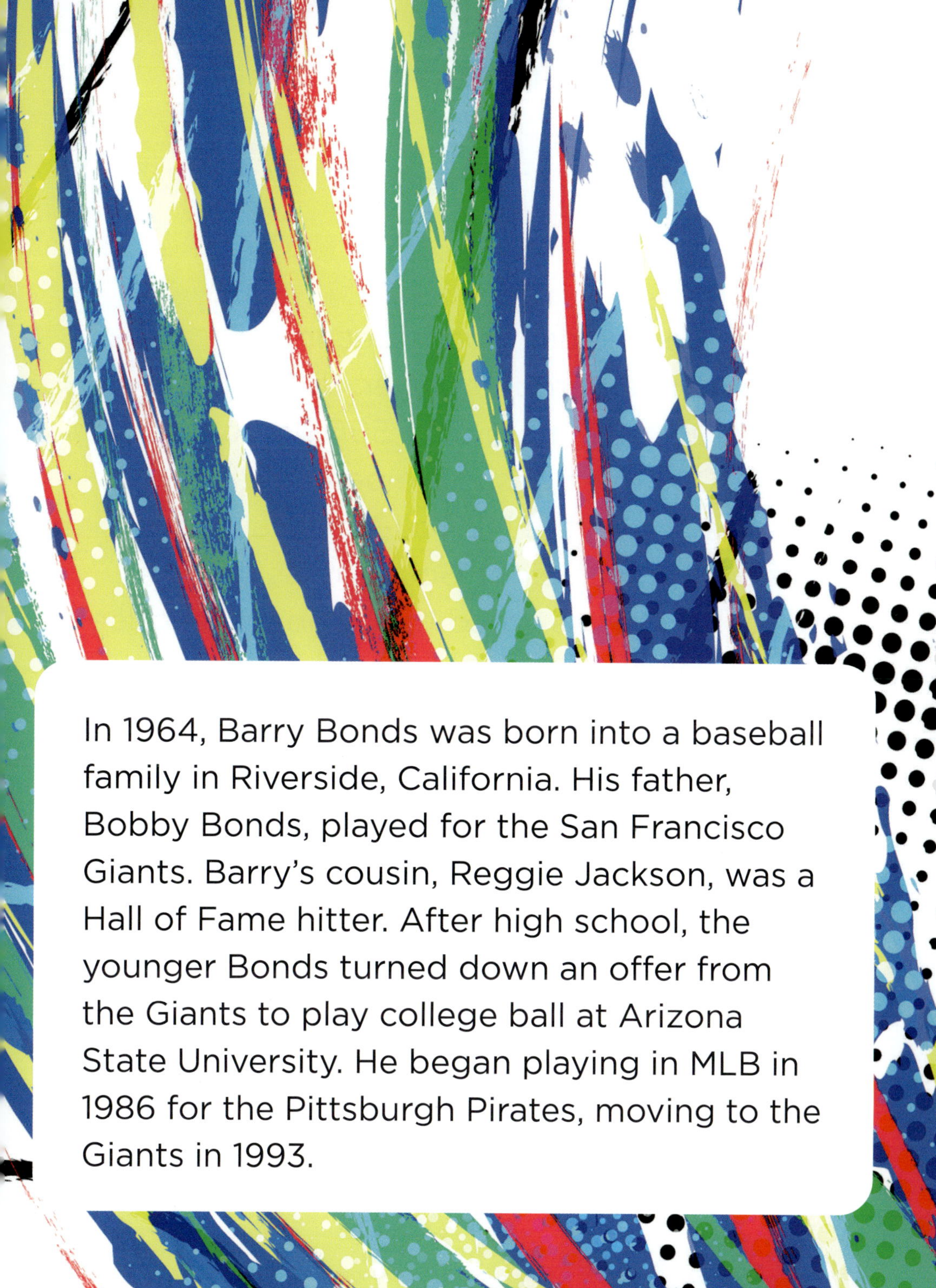

In 1964, Barry Bonds was born into a baseball family in Riverside, California. His father, Bobby Bonds, played for the San Francisco Giants. Barry's cousin, Reggie Jackson, was a Hall of Fame hitter. After high school, the younger Bonds turned down an offer from the Giants to play college ball at Arizona State University. He began playing in MLB in 1986 for the Pittsburgh Pirates, moving to the Giants in 1993.

CHAPTER FOUR

As a left fielder, Bonds became a legendary all-around player. He is the only player to have more than 500 home runs and 500 stolen bases. He passed Rickey Henderson as the MLB all-time walks leader. He won eight Gold Gloves for fielding. He was voted the National League Most Valuable Player seven times, making him the only player to win more than three times in either league.

However, Bonds is most famous for his home runs. In 2001, the left-hander hit 73 home runs, breaking Mark McGwire's 1998 record of 70. Bonds was on the way to a career home-run record.

Barry Bonds set several records during his MLB career.

CHAPTER FOUR

In June 2003, rumors of a possible connection between Bonds and the use of **steroids** began spreading. He testified before a grand jury that he had never knowingly used steroids. But when his personal trainer pleaded guilty to distributing banned steroids in 2005, it fueled the rumors.

Bonds kept going despite the situation. He passed Babe Ruth in career home runs in 2006. Then on August 7, 2007, Bonds faced pitcher Mike Bacsik from the Washington Nationals with a full count. Bacsik threw a fastball. Bonds connected, and immediately threw his hands in the air. He knew he had just broken the career home-run total record. He ended the season with 762 home runs.

Hank Aaron

Whose Record Did Barry Bonds Beat?

Hank Aaron was born in Mobile, Alabama, in 1934. He began his career playing in the Negro American League. In 1954, he joined MLB playing for the Milwaukee Braves, which moved to Atlanta in 1965. The right-fielder was a champion hitter. But as he approached Babe Ruth's record of 714 home runs, Aaron received racial threats. He broke the record on April 8, 1974, and ended his career with 755 home runs in 1976. Aaron received the Presidential Medal of Freedom in 2002 for his work in civil rights.

But Bonds's baseball career promptly ended. In November 2007, he was **indicted** for giving a misleading answer and lying under oath during his 2003 grand jury testimony. The Giants decided not to renew his contract. In 2011, a jury sentenced him to thirty days of house arrest for the misleading answer. They did not reach a verdict regarding lying under oath. The case against him was overturned in 2015, leaving Bonds with a clean record.

Bonds was **inducted** into the Pittsburgh Pirates Hall of Fame in 2024. However, he was not voted into the National Baseball Hall of Fame because of the suspected drug use. There remains a possibility that he could be voted into that organization in 2026. Three-time All-Star David Justice was quoted on Fox Sports in 2024 about whether Bonds should be in the National Baseball Hall of Fame. "If you want to put an asterisk on everything he did after 1998, fine, but you cannot tell me this man was not a Hall of Famer already."

Many fans believe Bonds should be inducted into the National Baseball Hall of Fame.

Aaron Judge

Chasing Bonds's Record

Aaron Judge grew up in Linden, California. He played college baseball for the Fresno State Bulldogs until joining the New York Yankees in the minor leagues in 2013. His MLB career began three years later. In the 2024 season, Judge increased his career home runs to 315. He signed a contract for nine more seasons with the Yankees in 2022, giving him potential time to beat Bonds's career home runs.

CHAPTER FIVE

Ichiro Suzuki's 262 HITS IN ONE SEASON

Ichiro Suzuki was born in Kasugai, Japan, in 1973. He joined a Japanese Pacific League baseball team after high school. In 2001, he came to the United States to play for the Seattle Mariners. Suzuki quickly proved that the hard pitches thrown by American pitchers made no difference with his .350 batting average. He won the American League Rookie of the Year Award and a Gold Glove for fielding. In 2019, Benjamin Hoffman wrote in *The New York Times*, “Suzuki was a top-notch defender and an above-average base stealer, giving him a skill set that sticks out among his peers.”

CHAPTER FIVE

On October 1, 2004, Suzuki faced pitcher Ryan Drese of the Texas Rangers in the sixth inning. He hit a hard single up the middle, giving him a record 258 hits for the season. Fans cheered as Suzuki was mobbed by his teammates. He then walked over to shake hands with the family of George Sisler, the man who's eighty-four-year-old record he had just broken. He later brought the record to 262 hits in a single season.

Suzuki had a bad year in 2011, and was traded to the New York Yankees the next year. In 2015, he moved to the Miami Marlins. Then in 2018, he rejoined the Mariners before retiring in 2019.

Suzuki started and ended his MLB career as a Seattle Mariner.

Suzuki's unbreakable record was due to superb hitting, but also to other elements of the game. He batted at the top of the order, making him one of only four players in history to have had 700 or more at-bats in one season. He took few walks. Plus, he had the stamina to play almost every game.

Suzuki will be eligible for the National Baseball Hall of Fame for the first time in 2025. Elliot Kalb wrote about Suzuki in an article for MLB in 2018. Kalb stated, "In an era of home run hitters, Ichiro showed us one could be a star with **bunts**, infield hits and stolen bases."

The New Baseball

In 2023, MLB made several changes to shorten the game. One was to put time clocks on pitching. Pitchers now have 15 seconds to throw a pitch with the bases empty or 20 seconds with a batter on base. These new rules could affect future records.

Whose Record Did Ichiro Suzuki Break?

George Sisler was born in 1893 in Ohio. He played baseball and other sports at the University of Michigan before he began pitching for the St. Louis Browns in 1915. Sisler changed to playing first base. He thought that once being a pitcher made him a better hitter. "I used to . . . study the batter and wonder how I could fool him," the National Baseball Hall of Fame quotes him as saying. Sisler hit his record 257 hits in one season in 1920.

In 2024, MLB revised its policy to include statistics from 1920 to 1948 for seven Negro Leagues in the official MLB records. The Negro Leagues formed because MLB was segregated, meaning separated by race, before 1947. This was when Jackie Robinson broke the color barrier by joining the Brooklyn Dodgers. The records of 2,300 Negro League players were added to the MLB official record. This data has changed some records in the sport. For example, Josh Gibson's career batting average of .372 moved him past Ty Cobb's record. Gibson also had a career **slugging** percentage of .718, moving him past Babe Ruth.

Sometimes rules change. Sometimes new players accomplish amazing feats. Only time will tell whose baseball records will fall and whose records will remain unbroken.

Jackie Robinson became the first Black MLB player on April 15, 1947.

CHAPTER FIVE

Luis Arraez

Chasing Suzuki's Record

Luis Arraez was born in 1997 in San Felipe, Venezuela. The San Diego Padres infielder has also played for the Minnesota Twins and Miami Marlins. Arraez has one of the highest batting averages in MLB. His sister gave him the nickname *La Regadera*, which in Spanish means "the sprinkler." It is a nod to his ability to put his line drives anywhere on the field. Arraez's consistent base hits give him a chance to break the record batting average, and perhaps Suzuki's record.

Think FAST!

Test your new knowledge of baseball by answering the following questions.

1. **Who set the record for most home runs in one season?**
   - A. Bobby Bonds
   - B. Barry Bonds
   - C. Reggie Jackson

2. **Why was Rickey Henderson nicknamed the Man of Steal?**
   - A. He was physically stronger than most other players.
   - B. He rarely struck out at bat.
   - C. He was especially good at stealing bases.

3. **Who set the record for career innings pitched?**
   - A. Cy Young
   - B. Corbin Carroll
   - C. Pete Rose

4. **Who set the record for number of hits in one season?**
   - A. Lou Brock
   - B. Joe DiMaggio
   - C. Ichiro Suzuki

5. **Why did Hank Aaron receive the Presidential Medal of Freedom?**
   - A. His 714 career home runs
   - B. His time in the military
   - C. His contributions to civil rights

Answers: 1. B 2. C 3. A 4. C 5. A

Glossary

acumen
Depth of perception

balk
An illegal pitching movement to fake a pitch

bunts
Gentle hits of a baseball to make it more difficult to field

changeup
A deceptively slow pitch

consecutive
Directly following another instance

indicted
Formally charged with a crime

inducted
Formally admitted into an organization

perspective
A different point of view

pick off
To throw out a base runner who is off base

slugging
A statistic that measures the total number of bases a hitter gets per bat

stamina
The ability to endure prolonged mental or physical stress

steroids
Performance-enhancing drugs

Find Out More

IN PRINT

Chandler, Matt. *Baseball's Origin Story*. Capstone Press, 2025.

Donnelly, Patrick. *Basketball Records That Will Be Tough to Beat*. Mitchell Lane Publishers, 2026.

Smith, Charles R. *Black Diamond Kings: Heroes of Negro League Baseball*. Candlewick, 2025.

ON THE INTERNET

"Baseball," ***Sports Illustrated Kids*****, n.d.**
www.sikids.com/baseball.

"Play Ball," ***MLB*****, n.d.**
www.mlb.com/play-ball.

National Baseball Hall of Fame**, n.d.**
https://baseballhall.org/hall-of-fame.

Index

About the Author

Cynthia Kennedy Henzel has degrees in education and geography. She has written more than 100 books for young people on subjects including history, geography, social issues, culture, and biographies. During her travels, she enjoys learning about sports that are less common in the United States, such as rugby and cricket.